CW01456093

IF SO, TELL ME

IF SO, TELL ME

Barbara Guest

REALITY STREET EDITIONS
1999

Published by
REALITY STREET EDITIONS
4 Howard Court, Peckham Rye, London SE15 3PH

Copyright © Barbara Guest 1999

Front cover art by Anne Dunn
Book design by Ken Edwards

Acknowledgement is made to the following publications in which
some of these poems first appeared: *The American Poetry Review,
Best American Poetry 1995, Conjunctions, The Columbia Review,
The Denver Quarterly, New American Poetry, The Partisan Review,
PN Review, The Poetry Project* and Z Editions.

Printed & bound in Great Britain
by Doveton Press, Bristol

A catalogue record for this book is available from the British
Library

ISBN: 1-874400-16-4

Eastern Arts
Board Funded

Contents

Valorous Vine

Lifts a spare shadow
                    encircling vine,
does not tarnish   bauble
     from overseas   and out of silver mine,
drop in clamor and volume.

Along the footpath
returned to mourning a lost stem,

gauzy the stem-like saving, or ruled
over stone to develop muscular difficulty.

In the wind
and overhead, held back lightning. Did
not surrender or refuse visibility and pliancy obtained.

Or confuse VIOLETRY with stone
or dissipate the land   land unshackled,
budding in another country
while dark here.

ii

It can be seen she encouraged the separation of flower from the page, that she wished an absence to be encouraged. She drew from herself a technique that offered life to the flower, but demanded the flower remain absent. The flower, as a subject, is not permitted to shadow the page. Its perfume is strong and that perfume may overwhelm the sensibility that strengthens the page and desires to initiate the absence of the flower. It may be that absence is the plot of the poem. A scent remains of the poem. It is the flower's apparition that desires to remain on the page, even to haunt the room in which the poem was created.

Storytelling

(introduce pavement)
Old-fashioned people in clothes.

Passage to friendship   *(details,momentum.firefly)*
  wave "bye bye,"

idly unfolds.

        (dark,light,etc.)

        (separately, form,)

      indifferent combinations. *(jest,tears.)*

(Rhythm   upswing) (collision with serpent),

           repeat and repeat moonlight
               *as suspense,*moonlight.

Outside of This, That Is

An oyster, the fragrance,
floating dog   outside and shuffle through hunger,
once again nothing so difficult when it passes in front

December goes before the new year. A battalion
of festival   largely in place by the region's devotion,
a flannel embrace, as if over, the green flavor.

A feathery existential bower shall block
the rude flagon. A grape
centennial passed
                    then passed as taught,
crowded by hope in a corral or anonymous
by the grape barrel,   by the Ancients and
                    mixed the Novella with grievous
          destiny.

A frame lets in elsewhere, a fairie
flies through Bretagne,   or guessed she flew,
Romance let her in. Others walk outside,
plants that wait their copying into the future,
                                        that is.

In Slow Motion

Melting, the melt of snow into midnight,
preoccupied, half alive, an activity in slow motion
        still attached.

    Moves outside the text   into the dark *under text*

    with closed eyes, detached, unmodified.

                A starry adultness
   took other means

         to lengthen the text,
         by emotion,

         and arguably noise

   wooed in this chapter and

         each page of,
           O real life.

Doubleness

Robins' egg blue   passes into darker color placed its head,
   fluid blue ascends,   Distance unrolling.

  Continuous reel, as in allegory.

  Another landscape,
                darkly hinted,

                 rupture of distance.

Body in the field — beyond uneven brick,

meaning in advance of itself.

Tree — bronze birds — sitting in it.

Imagined brick,
                landscape toy.

Doubleness.

This elaborate structure around the text.

a n n u n z i a r e !

DORA FILMS (1913)
Elvira Notari in Naples
* * * * *

Virgil's body in a grove above Naples
and nearby a camera:

toothpick beside a platter of teeth.

The camera prepares an *explanation* into the sky and to climb.

The mind wanders inside.   The camera is nimble,

touched by fearfulness

becomes more pragmatic.   It needs chiarascuro (light-dark)

should peril approach.

Elvira Notari uses the camera hood when il destino enters

in knit cap:

    the visual depends on the visible.

    Virgil at Naples' harbor leaning on his stick,

              the power to see

  what is invisible
              the stick in a position of power.

  A slap of oars   *leads to the visual,*

  gyrating where it ends.

         A likeness   *to what is believed*

  is the poem.   *The camera takes us, momentarily.*

Lily

reaches the locked door and inside the scalloping
    remnants of leafing enlarged.

Truancy of will where she let it fall   where I found
you after the disaster   the place under the lattice
is a hollow place   did not   remove pollen   let you alone.

   Door, and outside leafing,

     corrects what is random.

      Moss on the lily pond
and not worried. "Thinking is not worrying."

* Wish it were set to music.*
A carriage ride through a wood
to visit the swan (Ladou, Ladou)

     Moussorgsky!

The Poetry Meter

Miner
            of miniscapes, Selector,

            bend your knee
to this handwriting.

A special timing
            of hand-held meter,
                  risky when used by buffoon.
      Earth-flavored
            experience says so.

            Phidias

            Futurism

            Hand-Held Meter

      "Nothing but a fine Nerve-Meter" (Artaud)

The Lull

The lull in rain
*   is green   where came*
this dispute   the lull

is flat when it rests on a hill.
When a comma falls,

or crown rolled.

When a legend
passed through rain,

lull of rock and shatter.

Part of surrendered air,
the goat-like view,

"The Residenz of Goethe,"

and four or five liters of rain.

Russet Flame

"If one goes beyond reality...,"
        began the woman at the window,
        clothed in russet drapery.

Winter blows under her door.
The Serenade Tchaikovsky composes is made of russet,
streaked with bolder flame.

        Russet russet   bandage of hair
              indeterminate russet,   redandbrown
Snowrusset window,

                    russetflame.

Unusual Figures

A person stands in the doorway. Someone
    else goes to greet him.

They establish a calendar of meetings,
        apricot color.

Once they arrived together
        in a cab
        of electricity,

cool heat, desert air.

The author attaches herself
    to those figures.
peculiar to her asking.

They are needed by the pageant of creativity!

The unusual height and
    dots of activeness.

Is it from the basket shrub?

Lightness of feet,
circle of grey, of green overlap.
                What language
    do they speak?

If So, Tell Me

I give you the unhinged sleeve
dropped the seam   it went onto our back
was fodderless.

Wilted, say, by the gravel road
who ran a mile with legs apart
            neck hanging and groupless.

Bird shadow crossing the room   leave the outdoors!
Earns a pittance of food on the ledge   mother
of ten eggs   the real bird   feeds on ices
      the shadow is ten eggs.

Do you wonder if a run on sand is better than inside
does this strike you as shallow does it tease aloud
      the action
            is part of a wing.

The building was added it grew from an arm   protruded out of
a thigh   the upper terrace is fighting   is divided.

To think of you turned inside
your garment rent you are appointed   apart from the rites
            lessened, as in a daring scheme.

You are beheaded
much cast out that rolls on the ground, toss out thread
of what worked
to use or unlearn.   If so, tell me.

The Luminous

Patches of it

    on the lettuce a geography
    on trucks brilliant noise

      on the figure a disrobing
      radiance sweaters dumped

on water,

weightlifting there in the forest clump
striking at the underbrush, digging
past the clumsy curve

skipping certain passages, taking off
the sweater.

That fir cone found its voice on the path
in light after the sun came out

the postcard illuminates certain features in the face
the notebook lying on the windowsill,
the spindle back, the broken stem, all richer,

niceties tend to drop, also words like "many
loves" come forward the surprise of white stars

and the boots step by amazingly on the dried rich clay.

He swings his racket after it the luminous
the ball nearly swerves into it

those ancient people learning to count
surrounded by it, every day,

and navigators noting it there on the waves

the animus containing bits there on its subject
perched like sails,

bright rewards for preparing to strut forth
like the diver there on the board forced
by his greed into it.

Many loves changes to many times falling into
the day's lucid marshes

a tap on the shoulder or a first grasping that
object full of sparks

the wilderness untangled by it.

The fierceness with which it forged its memory,
its daylight, its absence.

Yes to the point of damages,
yes to the stunning infrequency,
yes to encourage with repetition its repetiton,
yes to sober knowledge of its parsimony.

A few fir cones, sails, the stain removed,
blazes from the paper without lifting your hands.

Strings

Wing of glass in high up floating

stave of time, or weight,   ceilingless and

of crystal time
measured, measure of,

pulls own weight, and dainty

protest,

plucked instrument, voiceless hum.

Deception

In the long ago days   he might

take her cloak
and place it upon
            a hidden arm,   and things

            before our eyes   work out. She would
    find the cloak
                near her cloak,
        and walk
                as if supernatural.

This Art   and the long ago Art,

become a comparison with Reality.

Remain only themselves,

if she does not reveal the cloak.

She shall disclose herself (herself still pointing)
            essential to the hidden

possessiveness in back of a throat,

the double S of the word.

In the twilight a blue-throated bird
finishes his song, and Nature is hushed.

repercussions, *soundings*   turn a corner
      meaning the poem may despise, and conflict begin.

By what *soundings* does one arrive at the interior? *Deception's* use of
deception, a scale suited to its size. *Soundings relevant,*
     yet unpredictable, in depth of poem.

     practices of deception existing: to encounter   arm, and sun,
  cloak   did not have its own ambition until they *vanish and*
return.
    Meaning, also.

An original intention, if lost in its bindery eclipsed there and not sung

  instinct develops   coveted and heard,   allowed to develop, even
    to deploy or wander   if *glitter* is not abolished

                the horizon

          in back of her throat/

Athletic Writing

Athletic writing
  jumps hurdles I put
into rain over the next State odd forward colors
 become bearers of fact whenever written with verbs
 I put softening on the rim. forestry housing.

Faery Land

A cloud opens a ruin of cloud
        piece of grey
    lifted out and patched.

In faery land clouds behave and wands.

 They seek
when I am turbulent have lost the knack,
  beasts and autre pays   tapered claw
they bury
     my skin   go folk
         with my toys

     take a barge and go.

Winter showed   it locked the pheasant
in a yard around it went   I took no notice,

so long a race I have run in Faery Land.[1]

---

[1]Spenser

The Paris Lectures

"What was said, what is meant?"

The Paris Lectures

"Elegies within."
Fog-banked shell,
rotunda writing describes.

White of Oaru. *The Husserl Lectures.*

"What was said, what was meant?"

The Green Fly

Orphaned caught in a web
the green fly.

No entertainment no grief

where they pick clover

the monument the soldier

goslings into new clover.

      More
   room   more
fur   more
          desire

to cross the winter day, a new magnet.

An excited misapprehension of *la Gloire*,

cheek of

brass.

Fought to the finish   stars

orchids, perhaps,

at dusk severely.

Multiple tunes   sunrise   gloaming

auditorium light.

Naked in thy boat.

Confession of My Images

The sliding window

left agape, and
the neck does not swell

an octave with ardor

is destablilized.

Of query and cultivation, of vases not known,
even as the known voice so is the alarm — .

Eros freed of the wooden seat

the crowd similarly, as

an elbow

fits into the ancient arm

touch
of sweet vest
creating furor.

to create sweet furor.

the page
                floats on knobbled water,

debris in the atrium,   "to visit Leopardi in Naples"

        supportive
                to breathe the same idiom.

Effervescence

Spill of ink, not enough
lather.

Ink spill
lather on the Rock.
Andromeda
long hair   nude body

NOISE
surrounds the painting   on the right side it is
cracked   the hair color changed   dried paint   altered the hand.
Wire is inserted into the gold frame.

Figures wait in anxious groups   distance takes away their height.
there is a furious
helicopter wind.

They lower a rope onto the Rock.
The painting is cracked,   her neck is chipped,
pieces of gilt curl fall off. She grows more naked.

Bone is exposed. The canvas mouth torn.

AIR IS PHOTOGRAPHED!

The wings of Perseus flap wildly,
his arm reaches under her.
He wants to lift her   A WING IS ABOUT TO FALL OFF
Strange to watch him holding onto his wing!

HE IS INAUDIBLE   the twittering
he makes blew it away.
The left wing is broken   his helmet remains.

Pieces of chipped paint litter the dock.

Memory goes backward and forward.

A painting by Ingres relates Ovid's story of the rescue of Andromeda from a rock
by Perseus.

The *Strum*

What is fraught and undenied travel in rare
dayishness supplication in ermine an approach.

        Landscape treated
to remoteness.

Newish place, ferns, gracefulness.

And excavation on
the edge of attendance.

        Weed dangle in hair.
Do not reverse shapes
go scared
        ermineless.

Ripe in default
what preceded
old root tree.

(detail starts to blur)

Nightingale
and human outline
landscape behind landscape.

Spill of ink not enough
lather
            bottomless
        passage in the *red strum.*

Dream of effervescence
pine and mountain gear.

a different appearance, new
imaginations
     here and beyond.

Music History

i

The rhythm of the section
nor said to be withheld
a credible garnering
a natural context of
    mountain property
nymph on the ground
fountain attached to
grotto.
    Mind you the soul of the piece
a tight operation
and viols
wilful counterpoint.
    Addresses the Mass
and far off Celtic tuning.
Wolf chorus
then bells lavender bells.

ii

Twittery business
at the waterfall
animal noise snow
snow cutting teeth.

The awe of
friendly speech.
Edenic viols
no promissory masterful
explanation of
the reprimand scene
a non-turbulent
withdrawal.
The camomile fades,
breeze off the lake
preparing lemon trees.

iii

Audacious idea
empty left hand,
Die Glückliche Hand,[1]
interrupts the idyllic shore-line
   light bulb
    mobility.

---

[1]The Lucky Left Hand, Schöenberg

Sideways

Sideways
become what is
    thoughtbred
and steeple.

Is true this bodie
has a surpass of beautie

thief in that heart ladle
ladle historic

        supergreen

printed in darkness.

No chill no vapor
unroll or unwarm
the skeletal

underground plenty
warmth of plenty
    is
        warrant.

Or gobble the soil

flavored

as if warm

ingratiatingly coated

invisible.

With sharpened

cornice

and is of

cheek bone

a tame animal

        scentsuet.

And tame animal

slungover his shoulder

wet autumn

of palette cloth.

Ennobled with surprise the root

deepens and the sprouting,

the pagan sprouting,

small packets of marble,

grains of it torture the eyes.

A greened-over tree years
                    (mourning)
of mourning and exploding.

of altering!

of 'unmudied visage'

(sideways

ALSO BY BARBARA GUEST

The Location of Things (1960)

Poems: The Location of Things; Archaics;
The Open Skies (1962)

The Blue Stairs (1968)

Moscow Mansions (1973)

The Countess from Minneapolis (1976)

Seeking Air [fiction] (1977)

The Türler Losses (1979)

Biography (1980)

Quilts (1981)

Herself Defined: The Poet HD and
Her World [biography] (1984)

Fair Realism (1989)

Defensive Rapture (1993)

Selected Poems (1995)

Quill Solitary, Apparition (1996)

Etruscan Reader VI
[with Robin Blaser & Lee Harwood] (1998)

The Complete Trees (1999)

COLLABORATIONS WITH ARTISTS

I Ching, with Sheila Isham (1969)

Musicality, with June Felter (1988)

The Nude, with Warren Brandt (1989)

The Altos, with Richard Tuttle (1995)

Stripped Tales, with Anne Dunn (1995)

OTHER TITLES PUBLISHED BY REALITY STREET EDITIONS:

Nicole Brossard: *Typhon Dru*
Cris Cheek/Sianed Jones: *Songs From Navigation*
Kelvin Corcoran: *Lyric Lyric*
Ken Edwards: *Futures*
Allen Fisher: *Dispossession and Cure*
Susan Gevirtz: *Taken Place*
Fanny Howe: *O'Clock* (O/P)
Sarah Kirsch: *T*
Maggie O'Sullivan: *In the House of the Shaman* (O/P)
Denise Riley: *Mop Mop Georgette* (O/P)
Peter Riley: *Distant Points* (O/P)
Lisa Robertson: *Debbie: an Epic*
Maurice Scully: *Steps*

Out of Everywhere: linguistically innovative poetry by women in North America & the UK (ed. by Maggie O'Sullivan)

RSE 4Packs No. 1: *Sleight of Foot* (Miles Champion, Helen Kidd, Harriet Tarlo, Scott Thurston)
No. 2: *Vital Movement* (Andy Brown, Jennifer Chalmers, Mike Higgins, Ira Lightman)

Reality Street Editions depends for its continuing existence on grants from funding bodies, sales and subscriptions, and donations from the following Supporters:

Alfred David Editions
Dodie Bellamy/Kevin Killian
Karlien van den Beukel
Ric Caddel
John Cayley
Kelvin Corcoran
Michael Finnissy
Harry Gilonis/Elizabeth James
John Hall
Alan Halsey
Robert Hampson
Randolph Healy
Peter Hodgkiss
Fanny Howe
Romana Huk
L Kiew
Peter Larkin
Tony Lopez

The Many Press/John Welch
Peter Middleton
Drew Milne
Edwin Morgan
Douglas Oliver
Michael Palmer
Bob Perelman
Marjorie Perloff
Frances Presley
Ian Robinson
Will Rowe
Pete Smith
Spanner/Allen Fisher
Harriet Tarlo
Andrew Toovey
Keith Tuma
Marjorie Welish
4 x anonymous

If you would like further information about subscriptions, or would like to become a Supporter of Reality Street Editions, please write to the address on the reverse of the title page, or email kenedwards1@compuserve.com

Web site: www.demon.co.uk/eastfield/reality/